# THE FIGHT
# FOR RIGHT

# THE FIGHT FOR RIGHT

## STRENGTH FOR YOUTH IN THE LATTER DAYS

Deseret Book Company
Salt Lake City, Utah

Chapters 2 through 15 have been adapted from articles appearing originally in the *Church News* under the series titled "For the Strength of Youth."

© 1992 Deseret Book Company

**Library of Congress Cataloging-in-Publication Data**

The Fight for right : strength for youth in the latter days.
     p.  cm.
   Includes index.
   ISBN 0-87579-631-1
   1. Youth—Religious life.  2. Youth—Conduct of life.  3. Church of Jesus Christ of Latter-day Saints—Membership—Juvenile literature.  4. Mormon Church—Membership—Juvenile literature.
BX8643.Y6F54  1992
241'.049332—dc20              92-30245
                                  CIP

Printed in the United States of America

10   9   8   7   6   5   4   3   2   1

# Contents

▼ ▼ ▼

CONTENTS

## Chapter One

# WHY CHURCH STANDARDS?

Richard G. Peterson

A manufacturer of a certain brand of beer has produced a television commercial that shows four male friends gathered around a crackling campfire following a successful day of fishing. They each hold a container of the beer and agree, somewhat emotionally, "It doesn't get any better than this." The viewer can scarcely disagree. The glow of the fire in the gathering darkness, the pleasure of fishing, the camaraderie of the campers — all are pleasant elements in a wonderfully appealing scene. The implication is clear: drinking beer promotes happiness, good times, and wholesome fun.

Such invitations to partake of the evils of this world are incessant and enticing. Some of the most appealing commercials shown on television *are* those produced to promote the sale of beer. In these commercials, beer drinkers are attractive, energetic, and youthful. The actors listen to music, dance, laugh, flirt, and participate in good-natured athletic competition, always in pleasant surroundings — usually near a swimming pool, on a beach, or perhaps in a picturesque mountain setting. If the setting is not pleasant — it may be too hot — opening the bottle or can of beer is sometimes shown to result in a change in the environment. Snow flurries materialize or palm trees appear.

The producers of these commercials strive to make us yearn for similar experiences. Since the law forbids showing actual consumption of beer in a television commercial, the environment, the personalities, and the activities are all carefully chosen to convey the message that drinking beer will result in the same kind of enjoyment in the viewer's life.

We are subjected to hundreds, if not thousands, of these entertaining but deceptive vignettes each year. The truth is they are intended to promote the sale and consumption of a product that is a health hazard, that robs its consumers of the ability to control themselves physically and emotionally, that prevents them from exercising good judgment, and that creates enormous danger when its users attempt to drive after drinking it.

The world has made its evils available to persons growing up in every period of history. But today destructive elements are more blatantly advertised and powerfully promoted. Advertising agencies, media specialists, and psychologists have pooled their expertise to create effective commercial inducements to buy their clients' wares. Moreover, the advocates of evil things are often attractive, popular, and well-known public figures. For instance, celebrities father or bear children out of wedlock without apology or hint of embarrassment or shame, and many of their fans find nothing in their behavior to condemn. The world seems in many places to have lost its conscience concerning honesty, morality, and decency. Crime and violence are proliferating at a frightening pace.

All of this is part of a great ongoing battle — a battle that involves much more than beer commercials on television. The battle is being fought between the forces of good and evil. And what is at stake is the safety and preservation of our young people in the Church. The adversary is powerful, determined, clever, and relentless. As we have often seen, he utilizes all the tactics he feels will give him an advantage. He has no sense of fair play. His ambition is to enslave and destroy the children of Heavenly Father.

We must not be deceived. Prophets have always understood this peril and have provided us with warnings. Enoch was given this frightening vision: "He beheld Satan; and he had a great chain in his hand, and it veiled the whole face of the earth with darkness; and he looked up and laughed, and his angels rejoiced." (Moses 7:26.)

How can we see through the deceptions? What is right? What is wrong? Is there a standard on which we may depend? Is there a reason to resist evil and to live the principles of righteousness?

Yes! The Lord has given us standards — principles to guide us, protect us, and lead us back to him. For example, the Lord revealed this warning to Joseph Smith about the latter-day deceptions the enemies of righteousness would employ: "In consequence of evils and designs which do and will exist in the hearts of conspiring men in the last days, I have warned you, and forewarn you, by giving unto you this word of wisdom by revelation — that inasmuch as any man drinketh wine or strong drink among you, behold it is not good, neither meet in the sight of your Father." (D&C 89:4–5.)

Because the Savior loves us, he has given himself as a sacrifice for our sins. He has provided that each of us will be resurrected. There is a wonderful place prepared for those who successfully negotiate this life, keeping themselves free from the contamination of the world. The Lord has promised us, "If you keep my commandments and endure to the end you shall have eternal life, which gift is the greatest of all the gifts of God." (D&C 14:7.) He has also said, "Learn that he who doeth the works of righteousness shall receive his reward, even peace in this world." (D&C 59:23.)

These are compelling reasons to live the commandments and observe the standards we have been given. By doing so, we partake of the Spirit and experience the joy that is the object of our existence. (See 2 Nephi 2:25.) When we live clean and virtuous lives, we are not troubled by our consciences — we walk without guilt. We enjoy going to church, relate comfortably with our parents and family members, relish our friendships, feel good about ourselves, and enjoy the companionship of the Holy Ghost.

To help us sort out the conflicting voices that vie for our attention—to teach us the standards the Lord has given us—the First Presidency and the Quorum of the Twelve have provided the youth of the Church with a clear statement in the widely distributed booklet *For the Strength of Youth,* which was first made available in 1990. The booklet covers a dozen or more standards that if lived by youth, will both strengthen them in a world that grows increasingly wicked and preserve for them the blessings of the Lord. In the preface to that booklet, the First Presidency said: "We pray that you—the young and rising generation—will keep your bodies and minds clean, free from the contaminations of the world, that you will be fit and pure vessels to bear triumphantly the responsibilities of the kingdom of God in preparation for the second coming of our Savior."

In support of Church leaders and their efforts to teach our young people the principles of righteousness, the *Church News* subsequently published a series of articles, each of which examined one of the standards set forth in *For the Strength of Youth.* These articles were written by persons who love youth and who have expertise or experience unique in the area of concern.

*The Fight for Right: Strength for Youth in the Latter Days* is a compilation of those original articles. They are published here in the hope that youth, parents, and leaders of youth will use them in the struggle to withstand the world's evils—that we might win "the fight for right."

THE FIGHT FOR RIGHT

*Richard G. Peterson is an editorial assistant at Deseret Book. He earned both his bachelor's and master's degrees in English literature from the University of Utah. He has served as a regional representative, a stake president, a counselor in stake presidencies, a bishop, and a bishop's counselor.*

Chapter Two

# DATING

Ardeth G. Kapp

In the booklet *For the Strength of Youth* (Salt Lake City: The Church of Jesus Christ of Latter-day Saints, 1990), the First Presidency has provided statements to help young people govern themselves and make choices that will "provide countless blessings... including the gift of eternal life." (P. 6.) The first statement on standards concerns dating.

As a youth in the Church, your immediate concern may be over a date for an event this very week, and yet decisions concerning dating have something to do with generations long before our time and also future generations for years to come. It is a big decision! To date or not to date, whom, when, and where.

Let me explain. Our Father in Heaven sent one of his strongest spirits to earth. His name was Abraham, and you and I are his descendants. Through Abraham, the Lord was able to establish a covenant people. He promised, or covenanted, with Abraham that all his descendants who accept the gospel and keep his commandments will inherit the blessings of eternal life, the greatest of all the gifts of God. Those who are not descendants of Abraham are adopted into the House of Israel when they join the Church and become heirs of the covenant of Abraham, through the ordinances of the gospel.

When we fully understand the significance of belonging to the House of Israel and being a covenant people, we can better understand how choices about dating become a matter of eternal consequence. Eternal marriage (temple marriage) is the link that unites generations past and future and opens the door to eternal life and all the blessings our Father in Heaven has promised those who love him and keep his commandments.

Each one of us has a divine mission and an eternal destiny. But to qualify, we, like Abraham, must be tried and tested. We must be given our choice, our agency, and be proven in all things.

When making a decision, we need to consider the possible consequences of that decision. In dating it requires giving serious thought to your desires, goals, and dreams for the future. Will your partner in marriage be from the House of Israel or adopted into the House of Israel through membership in the Church? Will your marriage be sealed in the temple for eternity?

You are probably shaking your head and wondering if all this must be rehearsed and reviewed each time you consider accepting a date. Let me assure you this is not the case. Once you make a commitment to a temple marriage, you will "date only those who have high standards, . . . and in whose company you can maintain the standards of the gospel of Jesus Christ." (*For the Strength of Youth,* p. 7.)

Every choice is a narrowing, and we become the sum total of all the decisions we have made in the past. When you think about the future, the determination to make wise choices in the present is best achieved. You may choose to give up what you want now for what is of greatest importance to you in the future.

In the booklet *For the Strength of Youth,* a message from the First Presidency provides valuable counsel regarding dating. Youth are counseled, "Begin to prepare now for a temple marriage. Proper dating is a part of that preparation." The counsel is also given, "Do not date until you are sixteen years old. . . . When you begin dating, go in groups or on double dates." (P. 7.)

If you are almost sixteen and are invited to a special dance, and all of your friends, both members and non-members, are accepting dates, it is a real test. To go or not to go is the question. If you go, then what? If you don't go, what? If you choose not to go, you'll miss the dance, and you may suffer a hurting inside at a time when friends, popularity, and acceptance are so crucial to your sense of well-being. But it is a moment provided for enormous discovery about yourself, your love for the Lord, your obedience, and the use of your agency at a time when it really matters.

Self-confidence, self-esteem, and increased faith are the

rewards for obedience to the commandments. It may be easy to argue and say, "Well, if I'm almost sixteen, what difference does it make?" The matter at this point may not have as much to do with dating or the dance as it does with obedience. And obedience at one time can become a source of strength for more challenging decisions later on. When mastered in your youth the self-discipline required to be obedient when you have your agency to choose will assure promised blessings all of your life. Parents who clearly and consistently hold to the principles and standards taught by our church leaders while providing understanding, love, and support to their children will have a tremendous influence as youth learn to govern themselves based on correct principles.

A custom in some areas is that of going steady. This implies a level of commitment to each other, an expectation of loyalty to one person at the exclusion of others. This arrangement is detrimental at an early age because it limits friendships, and of even greater concern is the increased seriousness of the relationship. It increases the risk of developing intimacy, which threatens your obedience to the commandments and your loyalty to eternal covenants, and it imposes temptations, which Satan uses to get people under his influence and rob them of the blessings that come through obedience.

And now about the date for this week. If it is an invitation from someone who does not share your standards, or that comes before you are sixteen or that would take you to a location that does not provide a good environment, what will your answer be? This will be a test, and it often comes from your closest friends, whose approval you yearn for. It may sound like this: "How come you're not going? Everyone else is. It's not that bad. We're not going to do anything wrong. Do you think you're better than we are? What's the big deal? Our parents are letting *us* go. We'll help you talk to your parents." To the question from friends, "Why do you do what you do?" in your heart you will simply answer, "Because I am looking to the future, and decisions today affect tomorrow and eternity."

Avoid becoming too anxious about dating. A survey shows that over half of the young women who graduate from high school have never had a date. You may be one of these. But the number of dates need not determine your happiness. There are many wonderful things you can be doing rather than just waiting for a date. Learning to enjoy people and developing friendships can be exciting if you'll let it. A young man or young woman who has many friends seems to be the one who attracts even more friends. As you enlarge your circle of friendship, others will be drawn in. While you may not be dating, you will be sharing experiences, building memories, and having fun.

If you become uneasy about your social life and impatient about this matter, remember to talk with your Father in Heaven. As you pray, express the yearnings of your heart and seek direction. "Search diligently, pray always, and be believing, and all things shall work together for your good, if ye walk uprightly." (D&C 90:24.)

The position of the Church, as taken by the Prophet Joseph Smith, has been to teach correct principles and to let the members govern themselves. The guidance of parents and church leaders is an important factor in how young persons handle the dating issue. If children communicate openly with their parents and seek the Lord in prayer, they can be guided to make correct choices that will help prepare them for temple marriage and all the blessings of eternal life.

*Ardeth G. Kapp has a master's degree in curriculum development from Brigham Young University. Sister Kapp worked as a public school teacher and as a clinical instructor in the BYU College of Education. A noted author, she has served as general president of the Young Women and most recently as a companion to her husband in his calling as president of the Canada Vancouver Mission.*

# Chapter Three

# DRESS AND APPEARANCE

### Elder Jack H. Goaslind

In a letter to the youth of the Church, the First Presidency has said, "We want you to know that we love you. We have great confidence in you. Because of that, we talk to you frankly and honestly.

"We desire everything in this world for you that is right and good. You are not just ordinary young men and women. You are choice spirits who have been held in reserve to come forth in this day when the temptations, responsibilities, and opportunities are the very greatest. You are at a critical time in your lives. This is a time for you not only to live righteously but also to set an example for your peers. As you seek to live the standards of the Church, you will be able to reach out and lift and build your brothers and sisters." (*For the Strength of Youth,* p. 3.)

With these inspired words of love and counsel, may I

share some feelings relative to the example you are to your friends and those who know you as a Latter-day Saint. As you live the standards, you will "lift and build" those with whom you associate.

The second standard discusssed in *For the Strength of Youth* is "Dress and Appearance." In today's world, much emphasis is given to our dress and appearance. Unfortunately, some of the standards set by the world of fashion are totally out of harmony with the standards set by the Lord. Apparently some fashion designers feel that the more exposure given by the lack of clothing, by the tightness of the fit, or by the shortness of the skirt, dress, or shorts, the more appealing. How untrue that message is.

Several weeks ago, a beautiful sixteen-year-old visited with me after a fireside. I was very impressed with her appearance and her dress. She shared with me briefly her experience of having waited to date until age sixteen, and then her disappointment that no one invited her on a date. In her words, she felt "unattractive, unwanted, and unloved." She had waited so long for the "big birthday number sixteen," but when it finally arrived, she was totally disappointed. She saw others who seemed to attract young men and were always "having fun," as she supposed. Over several weeks, she decided that perhaps a shorter skirt and tighter jeans might help her situation, so she did what so many others do and shortened a skirt to see if she would attract attention. What was the result? She said, "I did get attention, but I finally felt so cheap and so self-conscious that I could hardly wait to get home and change back to the person I wanted to be."

Though it is sometimes less noticeable at first, young men also often dress in a certain way to attract attention. Acceptance and belonging are conditions that everyone enjoys, if we are honest with ourselves. Often, young men of today, in an effort to "belong" in a setting that at first appears attractive, may experiment with dress and grooming styles that make a loud, negative statement. The world would tell you that putting on tight jeans, leaving the top three shirt buttons open, displaying three days' beard growth, wearing the longish, wet-look hairstyle, and getting a pierced ear sets you apart as "trendy." If you could see yourself as others see you, however, you would know that the standards of the world do very little to enhance the image of Latter-day Saints.

This doesn't mean that your only style should be a dress shirt and tie, however appropriate this is for Sunday dress. It also doesn't mean that you can't wear clothes and adopt grooming standards that are popular and very acceptable in your school, neighborhood, or group. What we hope young men will achieve in their dress and grooming, however, is an expression of the clean, wholesome approach. Because everyone is different, you can be different from others without expressing extreme styles. You can dress casually, comfortably, and modestly without losing your identity and your individuality. And you will probably do it for a lot less money. "The way you dress sends messages about yourself to others and often influences the way you and others act." (*For the Strength of Youth*, p. 8.) Don't be unwise and dress to get attention. Usually, you will attract those from whom you would prefer not to have attention.

How pleased I was to hear the young woman referred to earlier say that she knew her Heavenly Father loved her and that if she lived the standards given to us by the Lord, she would find enduring fulfillment in her life. Young men and young women can and should begin now to adopt a standard of dress and grooming that makes a statement about the kind of strong, decisive, and clear-thinking individuals that they really are. I encourage you to dress in such a way as to bring out the best in yourself and those around you.

The counsel given in the booklet *For the Strength of Youth* is some of the best advice you can get regarding how to avoid extremes in clothing and appearance. Those extremes include "short-shorts, tight pants, and other re-vealing attire. Young women should refrain from wearing off-the-shoulder, low-cut, or revealing clothes. Young men should similarly maintain modesty in their dress. All should avoid tight fitting or revealing clothes and ex-tremes in clothing and appearance." (P. 8.)

If you don't have a copy of the booklet, ask your parents or bishop about it. Take time to read it and become familiar with the concepts it outlines. It's not "preachy" or "stuffy." It's just a simple and straightforward guide to the kind of style that Heavenly Father wants all of us to adopt. It's written in language you'll understand, and it can be read in a few minutes.

Dear young friend, we love you. We want you to be yourself—your best self. We know that you are bom-barded every day in your schools, in your neighborhoods, in your workplaces by television, movies, radio, and videos, relative to the things of the world. But we also know that you and your fellow Latter-day Saint youth are bright, capable young men and women who are being prepared to lead out in the home, the Church, government, industry, medicine, education, and through thousands of skilled jobs and trades that will make the world a better place in which to live.

Prepare for those opportunities now by learning that how you dress and how you appear to others will make a tremendous difference in who you are, who you are to become, and what you can accomplish in life. God bless you to make wise and correct choices about dress and appearance that will set you on the course of a happy, fulfilled, and rewarding life-style.

*Elder Jack H. Goaslind was called as a General Authority in 1978 and is a member of the First Quorum of the Seventy. He has served as a member of the Presidency of the Seventy and as an area president. He has served as a stake president and bishop, mission president, regional representative, and general president of the Young Men.*

Chapter Four

▼ ▼ ▼

# FRIENDSHIPPING

Robert B. Arnold

B eing a good friend and having good friends are important to all of us. George Eliot wrote about how it feels to have a friend:

> *Oh, The Comfort — the irrepressible*
> *comfort of feeling safe with a person;*
> *having neither to weigh thoughts,*
> *nor measure words — but pouring*
> *them all right out — just as they are*
> *— chaff and grain together —*
> *certain that a faithful hand will*
> *take and sift them —*
> *keep what is worth keeping —*
> *and with a breath of kindness*
> *blow the rest away.*

The First Presidency has given us excellent counsel concerning the influence friends have on each other.

"Everyone needs good friends. Your circle of friends will greatly influence your thinking and behavior, just as you will theirs. When you share common values with your friends, you can strengthen and encourage each other." (*For the Strength of Youth,* p. 9.)

An example of friends who shared common values is found in the scriptural story of Daniel, Shadrach, Meshach, and Abed-nego. These young men were commanded by an unfriendly king to eat certain foods that were against their "word of wisdom." Daniel asked instead that they be given food that was good for them. For ten days he and his friends were allowed to eat the food they requested. Their countenances became "fairer and fatter in flesh than all the children which did eat the portion of the king's meat." (Daniel 1:15.)

A modern example of friends who strengthened each other occurred in the lives of nine young men who lived in the same ward in eastern Utah. Barry Woodruff and his friends were active in the Church and participated enthusiastically in its programs. When they started high school, four of the nine young men began missing Church meetings and other activities, occasionally at first and then more frequently. They became involved with other youth in the community who had a negative influence on their behavior and their attitude toward the Church.

Barry and the other four boys talked about how they might help their friends. They decided to plan some special activity each week to involve their wayward buddies. They also agreed to do all they could to encourage their friends to keep the Word of Wisdom. The friendship that bound these young men together allowed those who were strong in the faith to encourage those who were temporarily weak. Eight of the nine young men later served honorable missions, and all were married in the temple.

The friendship has continued through the years. Each summer the nine friends and their families meet to renew their friendship and to recommit themselves to help each other in their quest for eternal life.

In addition to helping our friends live the gospel, the Lord wants us to treat everyone with kindness and dignity. When the Lord asked Cain where his brother Abel was, Cain replied, "Am I my brother's keeper?" (Genesis 4:9.) Today we hear the same response but in different terms: "It's none of my business." "I don't want to get involved." "I don't care!" "If they're not into church, that's up to them."

On the other hand, King Benjamin taught, "When ye are in the service of your fellow beings ye are only in the service of your God." (Mosiah 2:17.) The First Presidency has advised us to "invite your nonmember friends to Church activities. . . . Help them feel welcome and wanted. Many nonmembers have come into the Church through friends." (*For the Strength of Youth,* p. 9.)

Great things will happen to us and our friends as we invite them to learn about the gospel and come to church activities with us. The experience of Alinda Allen and Lisa Greentree Miner illustrates the blessing we receive through sharing the gospel. Alinda loved Brother David Robinson's seminary class and wanted Lisa, her nonmember friend, to be part of the love and spirit she felt in the

21

class. Alinda told Lisa about the class and encouraged her to enroll. At the semester break, Lisa's schedule changed, allowing her to take seminary with Alinda. Lisa enjoyed the class very much.

As time passed, Alinda prayed often that she would know how to help her friend know the truth. She gave Lisa a copy of the Book of Mormon and encouraged her to read and pray about it. Alinda said she had "perfect faith" that Lisa would receive an answer. However, it was some time before anything happened.

One night, Lisa was praying hard for a witness that the gospel was true. That same night, as Brother Robinson prepared his lesson, he felt impressed to share a scripture with his class about Joseph Smith's struggle to know the truth. When Lisa heard Brother Robinson read the scripture the next day in seminary, she turned to Alinda and asked how the Church got started. They turned to the Joseph Smith story in the Pearl of Great Price and quietly read it together while the class went on around them. When the bell rang to end class, the two young ladies continued reading, right through the lunch period. As they read, Alinda received the most wonderful witness of the Spirit that she had ever experienced and knew that Lisa was being touched by the Spirit also. As they walked back to school together, Lisa said, "I think I believe this is true."

Lisa received the missionary discussions with Alinda and her family in attendance. As Lisa's understanding and testimony grew, she asked her mother for permission to be baptized. Skeptical of Lisa's newfound faith, her mother suggested that Lisa spend some time in Iowa with her grandmother. Lisa took her mother's advice, and spent two wonderful months discussing religion with her grandmother. During these discussions, Lisa discovered she could defend the things she had come to believe. Several weeks after returning to Utah, Lisa was baptized. Three years later Alinda experienced the joy of being with Lisa when Lisa was married in the Salt Lake Temple. They are still close friends.

Lisa is currently serving as president of the Young Women in her ward. As she works with the youth, she often refers to her journal and shares with them the entries she made as she struggled to find the truth and enjoyed the influence of a wonderful friend. Being a good friend is part of living the gospel of Jesus Christ. It cannot be separated from other gospel principles. The light of the gospel can influence our friends as they respond to our sincere example.

President David O. McKay explained it this way: "Every . . . person who lives in this world wields an influence, whether for good or for evil. It is not alone what he says, it is not alone what he does — it is what he is. . . .

"Every person is a recipient of radiation. . . . It is what we are and what we radiate that affects the people around us. . . .

"If we think noble thoughts, if we encourage and cherish noble aspirations, there will be that radiation when we meet people, especially when we associate with them." ("Prayer . . . and He Who Radiates," *The Improvement Era,* April 1966, pp. 270–71.)

Let each of us come to the Lord and receive the wisdom and strength to be a good friend and to have good friends.

*Robert B. Arnold has been a member of the Young Men general board. He has served as a stake president and a full-time mission president. He graduated from the University of Utah and received a master's degree from BYU. Brother Arnold is employed by the Church Educational System as an associate area director. He has served the youth in many positions, frequently as a Scout leader.*

Chapter Five

▼ ▼ ▼

# HONESTY

Maren M. Mouritsen

In the beginning of the booklet *For the Strength of Youth*, the members of the First Presidency indicate that they pray that you—the young and rising generation—"will keep your bodies and minds clean, free from the contaminations of the world, that you will be fit and pure vessels to bear triumphantly the responsibilities of the kingdom of God in preparation for the second coming of our Savior."(Pp. 4–5.) I want you to know that I pray for you too. "Sure," you say, "you don't even know me. You don't know how hard it is to be good. You don't know how it is out here."

I know it is hard out there, and I do know a lot about you. I know because my business, indeed, my life, is young people. I sit with you every day. Often from early in the morning through late evenings. I know something of your challenges and also of your successes. In these few paragraphs, I hope to somehow break the barrier of pen and page and talk to you as though we were walking along the edge of a cool mountain stream. That is where I wish we were because I seem to think better when I'm out under the sun or stars, and I need to think clearly because I want to talk with you about something important — *honesty.*

The day was bright and beautiful, and I was headed toward the Maeser Building on the Brigham Young University campus to teach my Book of Mormon class. As I walked, I became aware of two young men just in back of me who were talking loudly enough to be overheard. They were discussing a minor car accident that one of them had recently been involved in. The conversation went something like this:

"Well it wasn't too bad, and I was lucky. No one got hurt. I didn't get a ticket, and my insurance covered the damages. And guess what!" he said excitedly.

"What?" replied his friend.

"I found a mechanic who will repair my car really cheap. For much, much less — in fact a couple of hundred dollars less — than the insurance company paid." This seemed to catch his friend's attention.

"No kidding?" he replied.

"Yeah." Then, there was quite a pause, "But now I don't know what to do."

"What do you mean, you don't know what to do? Get your car fixed."

"No, I mean . . . " and then came the question, "Well, I wonder if I should pay tithing on the money I saved?"

The question seemed genuine and quite thoughtful. I must admit that now they had my attention. Their conversation concluded with the young man deciding to pay tithing on the full amount of money he received from the insurance company.

So what's the problem? I think the problem is that they never got to the real issue; they never asked the right question. It seemed so obvious. But not for these two good, young men. I was again reminded that many, maybe even most of our problems do not have obvious answers but sneak themselves in between the lines of our life and reside in the subtle, grey shadows.

I had recognized the voice of one of the young men. In fact, I knew him quite well. Suddenly, their struggle became my struggle. It was as if something in my head said, "Wait a minute. You're on your way to teach about standing for truth and righteousness in a Book of Mormon class." I was now struggling with my responsibility in this evolving situation. After all, this young man was my friend. It would be easy to let it slide. They won't know I overheard them, I thought. In fact, I began to rationalize that I should not have been listening anyway . . . right? Oh, well, I'd just offer a cheerful, "Hello," and be on with the morning. I was now at the bottom of the stairs, and as I turned to offer my "hello," the larger-than-life statue of Karl G. Maeser, revered principal of the BYU Academy, loomed before me. It was as if he were about to leap right off his pedestal. When we talk about honor and honesty at BYU, we almost always use his quote; it came to my conscience vividly.

"My young friends, I have been asked what I mean by word of honor. I will tell you. Place me behind prison walls—walls of stone ever so high, ever so thick, reaching ever so far into the ground—there is a possibility that in some way or another I may be able to escape, but stand me on that floor and draw a chalk line around me and have me give my word of honor never to cross it. Can I get out of that circle? No, never! I'd rather die first!"

The Young Women Values have become a part of my life. One of them is integrity. Almost without thinking, I turned and invited my young friend to lunch. He probably thought I was crazy, but a free lunch is a free lunch, especially to a struggling college student. We ate and talked about the real issues, issues that had nothing to do with this young man paying his tithing. We talked of honor and commitment, of integrity and honesty. We talked about what my friend's responsibility was to himself, to the insurance company, and ultimately to the larger community—you and me. Finally, we talked about returning the unused money to the insurance company.

That day we both grew. It was not an easy conversation, but it was an honest mistake. Added insight was like a ray of sunlight for him. There came a peace, a self-respect, and an assurance that no amount of money could either buy or restore. Together we rediscovered the principle that dishonesty hurts not only you, but other people as well.

There are lots of ways to be dishonest. But there is only one way to be honest, and that is with full-frontal attack—head-on, right here and right now. Even though the promise is that we can know good from bad, the choices are not always easy. The real tests come in how well we respond to the often marginal circumstances. The choices we make when things are not so clear-cut often determine whether or not we have personal integrity and are truly honest.

Committed Latter-day Saints must live and accept the principle that we are expected to be honest and true. The world expects it of us too. A few weeks back, I had a call from the graduate school recruiter of a major university. The call was in reference to a student for whom I had written a letter of recommendation. Those recruiters know about the Church, about BYU, and what we stand for. He explained that they had a few more places to fill in their class and lots of good candidates. We talked of this young applicant's qualifications, but the final question was, "Is he honest?" I had worked with this student and knew him well. I was so pleased to answer clearly and firmly, "Yes, you won't find better."

A person's ultimate honesty is the measure of that person's character. When one builds a firm foundation based on honesty, one's reputation for integrity can withstand the test when modest errors in judgment occur. When our behavior flows from a well of honesty, we will be seen as trustworthy and we will be sought out for our strength of character. A clear set of personal standards, when practiced regularly, makes for a clear conscience. It is this inner sense of direction, this spirit of goodness, that protects and guards us from many of the tragic errors of life.

Although a lie may give you tentative, temporary advantage, it is not long-lasting and will only cause you future difficulties. Personal character based upon dealing honestly with others and especially with God will enable you to make difficult but correct decisions. How fantastic and wonderful it is if it can be said of you that your word is as good as your bond.

So, please be careful, very careful. Careful not to purposefully plan to be dishonest or to do wrong. Careful not to take advantage of others by lying. Careful not to try to cover up your mistakes with falsehoods. Careful to be honest with your parents and your friends so you can establish trusting, lasting relationships. If you make every effort to be completely honest with yourself and to do what you know is right, your reservoir will be full. You will be blessed, and you will have hidden strength when it is needed.

Be a leader. Do what is right, and live so you can be trusted. Be honest.

*Maren M. Mouritsen is dean of Student Life and an assistant vice president at Brigham Young University. She received her B.S. degree from Northwestern University and her M.A. and Ph.D. degrees from Columbia University. Sister Mouritsen has served as a member of the Young Women general board and been active in leadership positions in ward and stake auxiliaries.*

Chapter Six

# LANGUAGE

Marilyn Arnold

For most of us, language is as common as the air we breathe. Like air, it is simply there, available to us almost without effort. We usually assume that the rarest things rather than the most common have the most value, but that is not so with either air or language.

Without air we would perish physically, and without language we would perish intellectually and spiritually. In recent years there has been a good deal of justifiable concern about air pollution. I wish there were equal concern about the pollution of our language.

I remember when *Gone with the Wind* was first issued as a film. Nearly everyone was aghast to hear Clark Gable utter a swear word on the screen. I hear you chuckling out there, but your very chuckles confirm the decline in public language standards. Once taboo in public media, the expletive used in the film now seems harmlessly tame by comparison with other vulgarities and obscenities that assail us in popular television, music, books, videos, and films.

Don't be fooled into accepting whatever has currency. When vulgarity, crudity, and profanity become as common in our everyday language as pollutants are in city air, our spiritual health is imperiled. Especially if we are the ones using the polluted language.

When we were youngsters, one of the defiant little cries we used to fling back at a name-calling playmate was this: "Sticks and stones can break my bones, but names can never hurt me." My more mature judgment tells me that names and gossip can indeed hurt the one maligned, but I don't think it ever occurred to me as a child that the *name caller* might also be hurt by use of the offending words.

The Savior made it clear that the words we utter can corrupt us. He said: "Not that which goeth into the mouth defileth a man; but that which cometh out of the mouth, this defileth a man." (Matthew 15:11.) Neither the Pharisees nor the disciples understood what Jesus meant. Disappointed that even Peter missed the point, He explained: "Do not ye yet understand, that whatsoever entereth in at the mouth goeth into the belly, and is cast out into the draught? But those things which proceed out of the mouth come forth from the heart; and they defile the man." (Matthew 15:17–18.) Remember this passage, too, when you are tempted to convey a bit of gossip, or repeat an off-color joke, or to laugh at one.

We sometimes like to think that the way we speak is

no real indication of what is in our hearts or who we really are. We are wrong in this. The words we speak and the ways we speak them do shape and reflect our character. Brigham Young insisted that the tongue does not operate independently of the heart: "If there is nothing in the heart which governs us, and controls to an evil effect, the tongue of itself will never produce evil." (*Journal of Discourses* 3:196.) Words do not spring spontaneously into existence; they are the product of our very natures. They reveal our character. Good words issue from goodness in the heart, evil words from evil in the heart.

I remember a story my mother used to tell (she told wonderful stories) when I was a child. It was called "Mother West Wind and the Seven Little Breezes." The breezes were Mother West Wind's children, but since she was a "working mother" and had to blow the ships to sea and back each day, she worried about leaving her children home alone. In her absence one morning, a wicked green goblin tries to win the children's confidence and get them to open the door. They are wary, and won't let him in until he succeeds in convincing them he is a kind friend. Through prolonged effort, the goblin changes his speech, appearance, and thoughts so that the helpless children will let him in. The irony is that the masquerade takes root in him, and the formerly wicked goblin becomes what he had at first only pretended to be. He becomes their dear friend and protector, and Mother West Wind no longer has to worry about leaving her little breezes home alone. The point of the story is, of course, that the way we think and speak in large measure determines what kind of person we become. Changing the way we think and speak, and even the way we look, actually changes us.

Our language should reflect what we wish, in our deepest hearts, to be. It is easy enough to be profane and vulgar if that is our highest aspiration, but what kind of an accomplishment is that? On the other hand, conscientiously using respectful, decent, and thoughtful language can make us better people. It can also change the way we see ourselves, and it will certainly change the way we are perceived by others.

Of particular concern to us should be the way in which we refer to Deity and sacred things. How we speak of Heavenly Father and his Son Jesus Christ is a sure indication of how we think of them. The tongue, remember, is not an independent agent. In modern revelation the Lord has been explicit on this matter: "Let all men beware how they take my name in their lips." To use the Lord's name "in vain, having not authority" is to risk serious condemnation, for all sacred utterances "must be spoken with care, and by constraint of the Spirit." (D&C 63:61–64.)

Try to imagine, too, what an affront it must be to the Father and Son when we make a commonplace of their holy names. What if someone used your name that way? If their names are on our lips throughout the day, to express a dozen different angry, mundane, or even vulgar emotions or exclamations, how can we then address prayers to that same Father in the name of that same Son and honestly expect their blessing? If we are inclined to dismiss language, especially our own, as being of minor importance, we would do well to remember that in scripture the Lord himself is called the Word.

*Marilyn Arnold has been a professor of English and dean of Graduate Studies at Brigham Young University. She served as assistant to the president at BYU and was the director there for the study of Christian values in literature. Sister Arnold has written curriculum materials for the Church and has served on the Sunday School general board. Her articles have been published in both academic and Church publications.*

Chapter Seven

▼▼▼

# MEDIA

Bruce L. Olsen

The Lord counsels us to be aware of the evils and designs that do and will exist in the hearts of conspiring men in the last days. This warning could well apply to what lies in the hearts and minds of many men and women who now control the content of today's popular media.

As a stake president, I have heard remarkable stories of young women and young men who have had the courage to get out of "slime-time" situations. They have walked out of movies, left parties, turned off music videos, changed channels, and sometimes even changed friends.

I have also observed the tragic consequences when people compromise their standards and indulge themselves in the evils that are available in the media today. I have seen homes broken because of addiction to pornography. I have seen men and women forfeit their chance to be married in the temple. I have seen babies born out of wedlock. And I have grieved over those who have, because of unworthiness, been unable to go on missions.

Certainly the blame for all this sorrow cannot be laid totally on the media. But both observation and scholarly studies demonstrate that what the producers of media promote will frequently gain acceptance as the norm.

You are part of the media generation. You are growing up in an era that looks to the media for news, information, and entertainment. There is no doubt that your generation has the possibility of being the best informed of any that has lived. Coverage of the war to free Kuwait is an example of up-to-the-second information about an event.

Today's media can have a positive effect on you, if you choose carefully. Television programs, movies, videos, even rap can provide some wonderful insights into life, reinforce your values, bring new understanding, and allow you to experience tenderness, joy, and spirituality. These things can motivate, inform, educate, enrich, and entertain.

Of course, the opposite can also be true. Vulgar videos, foul language, taking the Lord's name in vain, obscenity, deviant sexual behavior, and violence have become the cornerstones of much of today's media fare. Just look at a few statistics:

• Youth spend about 23 hours a week watching TV. By age 70 they'll have spent seven years in front of the tube.

• American youth watch an average of 14,000 sexual references — not counting commercials — a year.

• Youth view 2,000 beer and wine commercials a year. They typically watch an hour of music videos on weekdays, two on weekends. About 75 percent of music videos have sexual themes, and 50 percent portray violence.

• A study by the national Coalition of Television Violence points out that by the time an American is eighteen years old, he or she will have witnessed 32,000 murders and 40,000 attempted murders on television.

• The percentage of R-rated movies has increased 61 percent since ratings began in 1968.

• Nearly 33 percent of all close relationships on TV involve conflict or violence.

• Male/female associations on TV tend to overemphasize the physical aspect of relationships. Couples tend to spend a disproportionate amount of time expressing love physically rather than through acts of kindness, sacrifice, and service.

• Teenagers listen to an estimated 10,500 hours of rock music—sometimes called "Raunch'n'roll"—between the seventh and twelfth grades.

• By the time a student leaves high school, he or she will have spent 24,000 hours in front of the television, twice the amount of time that will have been spent in the classroom.

The list of concerns could be expanded. But what is important is how your exposure to such stimuli affects you. You might feel that your family life, education, standards, and values make you "immune" to such influences. They don't. Dr. Fredric Wertham, a psychiatrist, notes, " . . . my work convinces me that no immunity exists. Harm is harm. . . . There may be defenses against a snowball, but there are not against an avalanche." Too many teenagers and adults want to imagine that exposure to sleazy media has no effect. They are simply wrong. What is portrayed as the norm in the media often becomes our accepted standard of expectation and behavior.

Pornography is another matter for concern. This generation is surrounded by it in the content of television programs, movies, magazines, books, billboards, and music videos. In many parts of the world, these things are openly displayed on the streets. It can scarcely be avoided.

Just as the Lord has warned members of the Church about the dangers of alcohol and tobacco, he has warned your generation about the dangers that are present in polluted media. President Spencer W. Kimball, in an address to the students at Weber State College, cautioned this way: "Each person must keep himself (or herself) free from lusts, from adultery and homosexuality and from drugs. He must shun ugly, polluted thoughts and acts as he would an enemy. Pornographic and erotic stories and pictures are worse than polluted food. Shun them. The body has power to rid itself of sickening food. [But] the person who entertains filthy stories or pornographic pictures and literature records them in his marvelous human computer, the brain, which can't forget such filth. Once recorded, it will always remain there subject to recall."

Only you can control what you view on the screen and what you listen to on the stereo. But you *can* control it. You may not be able to avoid being confronted by the negative aspects of media, but you can control to what degree you allow it to impinge on your life. I hope your parents are also trying hard to help your family establish television, music, and other media standards that will protect family members. Listen to your conscience and give your parents your support. Your cooperation and strength will be a great blessing to your family. In your own personal life, control the media. Don't let it control you. What it amounts to is slime-time versus sublime-time — you make the decision.

If the video is violent or lewd, turn it off!

If the movie is sleazy, walk out!

If the sitcom is portraying pornography, switch it!

If the book is raunchy, toss it!

If the picture or joke is bad, walk away!

If it is a "turn-on," turn it off!

*Bruce L. Olsen has been managing director of the Public Affairs Department of the Church. He has previously worked as director of corporate communications for Geneva Steel and in a variety of administrative positions at Brigham Young University. He holds both bachelor's and master's degrees from BYU. Brother Olsen has been a full-time mission president and a member of the Young Men general board, and he has served as a stake president.*

Chapter Eight

▼ ▼ ▼

# MENTAL AND PHYSICAL HEALTH

Thomas E. Myers and
David T. Seamons

I'm tired all the time. I can't stay awake in class."
"I'm fat, and I hate it."
"So we have a few beers now and then—is that so
wrong?"
"Nothing I do seems good enough."
These and hundreds of similar statements are heard
each year in our offices. We wish that you could sit with
us and listen to our patients. Many of them are young
people. They come to see us with a vast array of illnesses,
injuries, and discouragement.
A young man named Jim sat hunched over in a chair.
He finished his tragic story with these words, " . . . and
so he fired me." His head was in his hands. He continued,
"That's twelve jobs I've lost in the last three years. I'm
only twenty-two, Doc. I've got a little girl and wife to feed.

I just don't know what to do!"

Jim looked strong and healthy. He was neat, clean, and probably a hard worker. However, once or twice, at the insistence of some high school "friends," he had used hard drugs. The drugs had damaged his brain, and he had become subject to drug hallucinations. Another unexpected hallucination occurred the previous week while he was working as a cook. He went berserk. In the short minute or two of the flashback, he had damaged some property and forfeited yet another job.

At the conclusion of our day, after the last patients are gone, we could sit and talk with you about the suffering we have seen. You might be surprised to see so many unhappy people. Even so, we would testify to you that the Lord's plan in providing bodies for us was "that [we] might have joy." (2 Nephi 2:25.) Jesus Christ endured so much to keep us from suffering needlessly. (See 1 Peter 3:18.)

Many illnesses (both mental and physical) come from self-indulgence and sin. We are taught that our bodies are temples, and as followers of Christ, we *must not* defile our "temple of God." (1 Corinthians 3:17.) Since our physical bodies are so important, it is not surprising that many of the temptations of today have to do with the flesh. Happiness and joy come from obedience to the principles that the Savior, not the world, has set.

People of the world boldly proclaim, "Eat, drink, and be merry, for tomorrow we die." (2 Nephi 28:7.) But the Lord gently suggests, "Strong drinks are not for the belly" (D&C 89:7), and, "If there be no righteousness there be no happiness" (2 Nephi 2:13). The world further boasts that true happiness comes from doing your own thing. The Lord states that happiness comes from obedience to the commandments of God. (See Mosiah 2:41.) It is obvious that man's ways are not God's ways and that what the world offers will only be counterfeit at best.

The following points are part of the code of conduct that the Lord has given us, a code of conduct that will lead to a happier life:

• *Avoid alcohol and other drugs.*

The Lord has counseled us specifically against the use of such drugs as alcohol and tobacco, including cigarettes, snuff, chewing tobacco, cigars, and pipe tobacco. (See D&C 89; 136:24; 1 Corinthians 6:10; Isaiah 5:22.) Hard drugs, wrongful use of prescription drugs, and even coffee and tea can destroy our physical, mental, and spiritual well-being. (See *For the Strength of Youth,* p. 13.) The Lord will not command in all things, so we should seek to use wisdom and moderation regarding the things that we take into our bodies.

• *Sleep.*

In teaching about sleep, Heavenly Father mentions two extremes. It is not good to either sleep too much *or* too little. "Cease to sleep longer than is needful; retire to thy bed early, that ye may not be weary; arise early, that your bodies and your minds may be invigorated." (D&C 88: 124.) He also reminds us, "Do not ... labor more than you have strength." (D&C 10:4.) You have probably discovered that when you regularly sleep eight to nine hours every night, you feel good, you get sick less often, and you are able to stay alert. Too much or too little sleep can leave the body weakened and the mind dull.

• *Exercise.*

Regular exercise is a must! Our bodies quickly lose tone, muscle, and energy when we do not exercise. The *kind* of exercise does not matter as much as the *frequency* of exercise. We suggest that exercise be done three or more times a week to maximize fitness. You may feel more motivated to exercise with a friend or with a group.

• *Nutritious meals.*

Social pressures to be the "right" size and shape often cause us to compromise our eating habits. It is wise to avoid fad diets. Be careful not to exclude certain foods, and be equally cautious about eating excessive amounts of food. It has become relatively simple to eat correctly. For most of us, good food is usually available, and basic nutrition is easy to learn. Nearly every LDS youth knows *what* to eat; the hard part is making the *choice* to eat correctly.

Again, the instructions the Lord has given us are specific. The creator of our bodies certainly knows best what will keep us healthy. His suggestion is that we use prudence in our meals, that we eat sparingly and with thanksgiving. Fruits, vegetables, meats, and grains are all part of a balanced diet. (See D&C 89; Genesis 1–2; Abraham 5:9.)

• *Mental health.*

To feel joy and happiness is our goal. (See 2 Nephi 2:25.) Thoughts that are hopeful, lots of good humor, and an optimistic outlook all contribute to good mental health. Uplifting music, scripture study, faith in God, and goal setting are basic elements to happiness. Behaving selfishly, judging and criticizing others, and indulging in self-pity are sure to bring depression and sadness. Let us avoid this kind of destructive behavior. We now know that we can learn how to control our thoughts and many of our emotions. As we take control of our thoughts, we are less subject to the ideas and moods of others.

For many young people who come into our offices, life is a battle. It need not be! Jesus Christ compassionately invites each of us to come unto him and promises that our burdens can be made light. (See Moroni 10:32; Matthew 11:29–30.) He has also provided us a plan as outlined in *For the Strength of Youth*. Keeping our bodies and minds as healthy as possible allows us to function better as receivers of spiritual instruction from Heavenly Father. As we come unto Christ, we become more like him and prepare ourselves to be with him again.

*Thomas E. Myers is a medical doctor who received his degree from the University of Alabama School of Medicine. He has been an assistant professor at the University of Nevada School of Medicine and maintains a private medical practice. Brother Myers has been a high councilor, a ward Young Men president, and a bishop.*

*David T. Seamons received his bachelor's and master's degrees in psychology and his Ph.D. in clinical psychology, the latter from Brigham Young University. He practices marriage and family therapy. Brother Seamons has served as a ward Young Men president, a high councilor, a bishop, and a stake president.*

## Chapter Nine

▼ ▼ ▼

# MUSIC

### Michael Ballam

W hat a magnificent age in which to live! All the knowledge and understanding of millennia have come together to give us enlightenment and power. We can span the globe in minutes, venture into space, cure diseases previously feared, communicate instantly throughout the world, and share the art and culture of all civilizations in our homes and communities.

The notion that the valiant and great spirits of the Lord have been saved until the last days is a noble and happy thought. It is good news to think that we might have been "held back" to this dispensation for an admirable purpose. Yet, there is with that an awesome responsibility, for we have been positioned here for one of the greatest battles in history. It is not a battle yet to come, but we actually are in it now. It is an unfair fight, for we are on enemy territory, and our enemy's weapons are highly developed.

The battle of which I speak is the battle between good and evil, light and dark, love and hate. It is the current engagement in the war that began in the premortal life, and it is now building to a great crescendo.

The commander in chief of this enemy force is well known to us; we call him by many names: the prince of darkness, the deceiver, Satan or the devil. His power is great, and his weapons are mighty. One of the most powerful weapons in the arsenals of both sides is music. It has great power to further both sides of the conflict. For me, other than prayer, great music has been the best way to communicate with God.

Music is an important element in the work of the Lord:

• Angelic choirs sang on the occasion of the birth of Jesus Christ. (See James E. Talmage, *Jesus the Christ*, Salt Lake City: Deseret Book, 1949, pp. 93–94.)

• Jesus and his disciples sang a hymn just prior to his going into the Garden of Gethsemane. (See Matthew 26:30.)

• Joseph Smith was comforted in Carthage Jail when John Taylor sang, "A Poor Wayfaring Man of Grief." (See *History of the Church*, 6:614–15.)

• Emma Smith was instructed by the Lord to make a selection of hymns for use by the Church. (See D&C 25:11.)

• The second coming of the Savior will be heralded by music. (See Zephaniah 3:17.)

The Lord has confirmed his love of music in the statement: "For my soul delighteth in the song of the heart; yea, the song of the righteous is a prayer unto me, and it shall be answered with a blessing upon their heads." (D&C 25:12.)

J. S. Bach believed that the final aim of music was to glorify God. Many composers of sacred music attributed their inspiration to a divine source. Beethoven and Handel credited God, the Almighty Father, with revealing himself to them through their musical compositions. I think that the powers from which all truly great composers like Mozart, Brahms, Schubert, Bach, and Beethoven drew their inspiration is the same power that enabled Jesus to work his miracles. It is the power that created our earth and the whole universe. Do you know the music of Bach, Beethoven, Handel, Brahms, Mozart? In their music lies the chance to tap into great power: God's power.

Many of the masterpieces of music seem to come from the past. In trying to figure out the reason, I compiled a list of the works considered by the world as great classics, such as Beethoven's "Ninth Symphony," Brahms's "Requiem," Bach's "St. Matthew Passion," and Mozart's "Magic Flute." It was not surprising to me to see that the large body of such music was either written or discovered within fifty years of 1830—the year the Church was organized.

That was an age of enlightenment. The Lord was flooding the earth with light and knowledge, not only at the Hill Cumorah, but in science, literature, and music. He was, as both Isaiah and Nephi had prophesied, making "bare his holy arm" to all the world. (Isaiah 52:10; see 1 Nephi 22:10.) His voice can be heard in great music in the same way it can be heard in the writings of Isaiah, Moroni, Matthew, and Moses.

Throughout history, music has been described as the "language of the Gods." I am a witness to that principle. I have been blessed on many occasions to know of God's existence and power by performing, or by listening to, divinely inspired music. Hearing God's voice in music is a form of personal revelation and one of the whisperings of the Spirit. In the Old Testament we read about the positive effects of music: "When the evil spirit . . . was upon Saul, . . . David took an harp, and played with his hand: so Saul was refreshed, and was well, and the evil spirit departed from him." (1 Samuel 16:23.) Divinely inspired music *can* rid us of forces that vex us and bring us pain. Therein lies the power!

That is glorious news. It is also bad news, because the same principle works on the dark side. If music can drive away evil spirits, can the reverse also be true? Can certain forms of music *invite* evil spirits to provoke and instruct us?

Well-conceived and skillfully performed music can open our spirits to messages from the master of deceit and destruction. President Ezra Taft Benson warned that "the devil knows that music has the power to ennoble or corrupt, to purify or pollute. . . . His sounds come from the dark world of drugs, immorality, obscenity, and anarchy." (*The Teachings of Ezra Taft Benson* [Salt Lake City: Bookcraft, 1988], p. 326.)

I am also a witness of this principle. My own understanding of this did not come from reading others' opinions or listening to testimonies of others. What I know I have seen with my own eyes as I have spent my life in the entertainment industry. The great artists of the world have been my colleagues. I know them, and I know the source of their power. Many have boasted of satanic contracts and pacts. Evidence of that may be seen in the effect their music has on their listeners.

We are now in another era of enlightenment. The forces of good and evil are taking sides. The First Presidency has counseled us: "Shun music that is spiritually harmful. Don't listen to music that contains ideas that contradict principles of the gospel. Don't listen to music that promotes Satanism or other evil practices, encourages immorality, uses foul and offensive language, or drives away the Spirit." (*For the Strength of Youth,* p. 14.) Because music is so powerful, it can also carry messages of degradation and destruction that can take us to the very lowest valley. It is therefore vital that Latter-day Saints carefully choose the music to which they listen and that they use the Spirit of the Lord in determining the music with which they surround themselves.

During the war in the Persian Gulf we learned about a new type of weaponry—the Patriot missile—which has the power to disarm and destroy a destructive Scud missile before it has a chance to annihilate. This is the same sort of defense we must adopt in the conflict in which we are now engaged. We must disarm the power of darkness *before* it impacts on us by not allowing its power to infect us through music inspired by the dark side.

There is no longer time to be passive about the influences we allow around us. To make good judgments, we must surround ourselves with a shield of light that comes from the Spirit of God. Furthermore, we are promised "perfect knowledge" in judging the source of inspiration of all music. Moroni has given us the key to understanding. He states: "It is given unto you to judge, that ye may know good from evil; and the way to judge is as plain, that ye may know with a perfect knowledge, as the daylight is from the dark night. For behold, the Spirit of Christ is given to every man, that he may know good from evil; wherefore, I show unto you the way to judge; for every thing which inviteth to do good, and to persuade to believe in Christ, is sent forth by the power and gift of Christ; wherefore ye may know with a perfect knowledge it is of God.

"But whatsoever thing persuadeth men to do evil, and believe not in Christ, and deny him, and serve not God, then ye may know with a perfect knowledge it is of the devil; for after this manner doth the devil work, for he persuadeth no man to do good, no, not one; neither do his angels; neither do they who subject themselves unto him." (Moroni 7:15–17.)

Music that does not meet the criteria of inviting to do good and persuading to believe in Christ is not divinely inspired. Music that causes us to abandon our ethics, lower our morals, injure others, or even cause death is inspired by darkness.

One of the great testimonies of the Savior borne in my lifetime is the extraordinary witness of Elder Bruce R. McConkie. He said that great music is eternal, given of God to further his purpose, and that we may learn more quickly through music than by many other means. He also attested that many prayers have been answered through great music. (See *Mormon Doctrine* [Salt Lake City: Bookcraft, 1966], pp. 520–22.)

I have received a personal witness of the Lord's divinity through great music as well as through the scriptures. We must seek to hear his voice from wherever it might come.

*Michael Ballam is an associate professor of Music at Utah State University. A widely acclaimed operatic tenor, he has performed in the major concert halls of the world and has numerous recordings to his credit. He received his bachelor's degree from Utah State University and his doctor of music degree from Indiana University. Brother Ballam has served as a high councilor and special music missionary.*

## Chapter Ten

▼ ▼ ▼

# DANCING

Elder Stephen D. Nadauld

The booklet *For the Strength of Youth* provides guidelines and standards that can direct youthful enthusiasm and vitality into strength. Families throughout the Church are joining together in family home evening sessions or other appropriate settings to discuss with youth the topics that are treated therein. One such topic is that of dancing. In that booklet we are instructed that "dancing can be enjoyable and provide an opportunity to meet new people and strengthen friendships." (*For the Strength of Youth,* p. 14.)

For many, dancing is definitely fun. It is a form of self-expression enjoyed by people of all ages, but it is especially attractive to our youth, who are blessed with so much energy and vigor. The impulse to dance is a natural one and is even referred to in the scriptures. We learn that David danced before the Lord (see 2 Samuel 6:14) and that the Psalmist said, "Sing unto the Lord a new song. . . . Let them praise his name in the dance" (Psalm 149:1–3). More recently, Latter-day Saints were told in the Doctrine and Covenants, "If thou art merry, praise the Lord with singing, with music, with dancing, and with a prayer of praise and thanksgiving." (D&C 136:28.) We know the pioneers were fond of dancing. As Brigham Young led the Saints across the plains, they often danced by the light of the evening fire after the last work of the day had been done.

We can suppose that dancing means different things to different people. For example, dance forms vary widely from country to country, and from culture to culture. Some dance forms have developed over a long period of time, such as classical ballet. Traditional dances that are peculiar to specific cultures are called folk dances, and great effort is made to preserve and perform them with fidelity to original dress and music. Ballroom dancing includes many different steps and ranges from the graceful waltz to the samba and the rumba, which are performed to exciting Latin rhythms.

Some dance forms gain rapid popularity because of fads and then are quickly discarded. The Charleston from the 1920s, the twist made popular by Chubby Checker, and the surf from the Beach Boys' era are examples of dance fads that have captured the imagination of dancers and then died away.

What does dancing mean to Latter-day Saint youth? Let me share with you excerpts from two letters recently received at Church headquarters. The first: "I am thirteen years old, almost fourteen. My birthday is December 5. I am writing you this letter concerning being able to go to dances at my school. My parents have told me they don't think I am old enough to go. I want to know if you think it's all right if I go to the dances at my school.

"They are well-supervised and chaperoned. I would have my parents, or one of my friends' parents, take me and pick me up after the dance. I would not have a date, and I would dance with a whole bunch of different boys. I know this seems like it shouldn't bother me, and if you don't answer my letter in time for the Halloween dance, I won't go, but I need to know your thoughts and opinions on it. I love my parents a lot and don't want to disobey them! Please write back as soon as possible. Thank you for caring."

The second letter: "I would like to ask you a question. Our stake is really having a problem about the standards at our stake dances. How should we dance to the slow songs? This boy I know is pressuring me to dance in a 'bear hug.' Is this the wrong way to dance? Urgent. Answer fast."

These two letters demonstrate a remarkable and wonderful desire exhibited by youth throughout the Church to do what is right, to listen to the counsel of loving parents, and to seek additional insight from leaders.

Sometimes it is not easy to figure out what's right. But, let's examine more closely the questions raised by the two youthful letter writers. A rereading suggests that there are three issues of concern:

(1) Am I old enough to go? i.e., When is the right time?

(2) Can I go to a school dance? i.e., Where is the right place?

(3) How should I dance? i.e., What is the proper manner?

To answer these questions we need to understand some general principles and then try to apply the principles to specific situations.

In light of this, consider the following counsel concerning dancing:

First, because there are so many varied situations and circumstances surrounding dancing, you need to work out the specifics of time, place, and manner with your parents. (Parents take note: In order to give good counsel and advice, you need to know what's going on. Talk to your young people, talk to other parents, listen to the dance music, visit with dance sponsors, drop in to the dance for ten minutes on your way to or from your activities.) In other words, whether or not thirteen-year-old girls (or boys) can attend matinee, nondate, school dances should be decided in a spirit of love and understanding by girls and boys and their parents.

Second, some guidelines for Church-sponsored dances are found on page seven of *The Activities Manual*. They include the following: (1) Lyrics should not be contrary to gospel principles. (2) The beat of the music, whether instrumental or vocal, should not dominate the melody. (3) Lighting should be bright enough for people to see across the room. Strobe lighting is generally not advised, and psychedelic lighting that pulsates with the beat is not acceptable. (4) Music volume should be low enough so that two people standing side by side can hear each other as they carry on a normal conversation. Additionally, the *Young Women Handbook,* page twenty, advises that dress, grooming, lighting, dance styles, lyrics, and music associated with any dance activity should contribute to an atmosphere in which the Spirit of the Lord may be present. When we compromise these standards we invite a contrary spirit into our activities and end up imitating the worldly way of doing things.

Time will tell whether or not the "bear hug" will be an enduring dance style. At best it is a "default" position that comes from not knowing alternative positions and styles that can be learned. (Learning the graceful and appropriate ballroom dance styles can be as fun as learning how to play football, basketball, or how to be a cheerleader, and these skills will provide enduring enjoyment long after your jump shot has turned into a hop shot.) At worst the "bear hug" leads to thoughts, feelings, and possibly behavior that will only cause sorrow and heartache. So leave the bear hugging to the bears — try the foxtrot or the jitterbug or the bunny hop (ask someone over forty about this).

Finally, guidelines are helpful — pay attention to them and counsel with your parents. But in the final analysis, please remember that dancing is a form of self-expression that needs to reflect your personal standards of modesty and restraint. Good judgment and self-discipline apply in dancing just as they do in everything else you do. You know who you are and what you stand for. You're entitled to feelings about right and wrong. Pay attention to them, and you'll dance your way through a long and happy life.

*Elder Stephen D. Nadauld, a member of the Seventy, has served as a member of the general presidency of the Young Men. He earned a bachelor's degree from BYU, a master's from Harvard, and a doctorate from the University of California at Berkeley. He has been president of Weber State University. Elder Nadauld has served as a Scoutmaster, bishop, stake president's counselor, and regional representative.*

## Chapter Eleven

▼ ▼ ▼

# SEXUAL PURITY

### Elder John M. Madsen

It was my privilege to be present on October 13, 1987, in the Marriott Center on the Brigham Young University campus, as our prophet President Ezra Taft Benson delivered a devotional address. He spoke on the law of chastity. I wish all the youth of the Church could have been present to hear his message and feel his love.

He said, "From the beginning of time, the Lord has set a clear and unmistakable standard of sexual purity. That standard is the law of chastity. It is the same for all—it is the same for men and women; it is the same for old and young; it is the same for rich and poor.... The law of chastity is a principle of eternal significance. We must not be swayed by the voices of the world. We must listen to the voice of the Lord and then determine that we will set our feet irrevocably upon the path He has marked....

"I say again, as have all the prophets before me, there

is one standard of virtue and chastity and all are expected to adhere to it. What the Lord says to one, He says to all; 'Ye must practice virtue and holiness before me continually.' (D&C 46:33.)"

In the excellent and timely booklet *For the Strength of Youth,* the Lord through his servants has set before us the standards of the Church, including the law of chastity or sexual purity. We are told that "the Lord specifically forbids certain behaviors, including all sexual relations before marriage, petting, sex perversion (such as homosexuality, rape, and incest), masturbation, or preoccupation with sex in thought, speech, or action." (*For the Strength of Youth,* p. 15.) In the letter of introduction to that booklet, the First Presidency counsels and pleads with us to live morally clean lives, keeping both our "bodies and minds clean, free from the contaminations of the world," so that we will be "fit and pure vessels to bear triumphantly the responsibilities of the kingdom of God in preparation for the second coming of our Savior." (Pp. 4–5.)

There are other voices, the "voices of the world." They are the seductive, persuasive, "learned," evil, and always confused voices that entice us to disobey the law of chastity. (See D&C 46:7–8.) These voices would have us believe that to have "fun," to be "free" or "popular" or to experience "self-fulfillment," we must abandon all standards of sexual purity and decency. All such doctrines are inspired of the devil, the father of lies, who seeks to deceive and blind and lead away captive the souls of men. (See Moses 4:3–6.) The scriptures record the awful, bitter, tragic, and deadly fruits of sexual immorality. (See Moses 5:12–13; 7:33–34; Genesis 19; Jacob 2:5–9, 31–35; 3:11–12; Alma 39:5–9.)

We have before us the voices of the Lord and his servants, and the voices of the devil and his servants. Latter-day Saint youth, what is your choice? Who do you believe? Who will you follow in this matter? As Joshua said of old, "Choose you this day whom ye will serve." (Joshua 24:15; see also Romans 6:16; Alma 29:5.) As you make your choice, remember, you are free to choose! But you are not free from the consequences of your choices. (See 2 Nephi 2:27–29.)

Remember also: "You are a child of God. He is the father of your spirit. Spiritually you are of noble birth, the offspring of the King of Heaven. Fix that truth in your mind and hold to it. However many generations in your mortal ancestry, no matter what race or people you represent, the pedigree of your spirit can be written on a single line. You are a child of God! . . .

"Within your body is the power to beget life, to share in creation. The only legitimate expression of that power is within the covenant of marriage. The worthy use of it is the very key to your happiness. Do not use that power prematurely, not with anyone. The misuse of it cannot be made right by making it popular." (Boyd K. Packer, "To Young Women and Men," *Ensign*, May 1989, p. 54; see also *Gospel Doctrine: Selections from the Sermons and Writings of Joseph F. Smith* [Salt Lake City: Deseret Book Company, 1975], pp. 275, 309.)

"There is no lasting happiness in immorality. There is

no joy to be found in breaking the law of chastity. Just the opposite is true. There may be momentary pleasure. For a time it may seem like everything is wonderful. But quickly the relationship will sour. Guilt and shame set in. We become fearful that our sins will be discovered. We must sneak and hide, lie and cheat. Love begins to die. Bitterness, jealousy, anger, and even hate begin to grow. All of these are the natural results of sin and transgression.

"On the other hand, when we obey the law of chastity and keep ourselves morally clean, we will experience the blessings of increased love and peace, greater trust and respect for our marital partners, deeper commitment to each other, and, therefore, a deep and significant sense of joy and happiness." (Ezra Taft Benson, Devotional Address, BYU, October 13, 1987.)

Because you are a child of God, "in dating, [you should always] treat your date with respect, and expect your date to show that same respect to you." (*For the Strength of Youth*, p. 15.) As part of the generation enjoying the fullness of the gospel, you ought to see clearly that "the wages of sin is death," both spiritual and physical. (Romans 6:23.)

Like faith, obedience to the law of chastity or sexual purity is a fundamental requirement for entering the celestial kingdom. (See 2 Peter 1:4–10.) All who are not willing to obey "the law of Christ," or the law of the celestial kingdom, "cannot abide a celestial glory." They will thus forfeit the right to have a celestial body, for only "they who are of a celestial spirit" shall receive a celestial body, with all its sacred powers, privileges, and blessings. (See D&C 88:20–22, 28; 93:33.)

We must never be deceived into thinking that it is "no big deal" to engage in sexual sins or that these are things from which we can quickly repent. Satan knows these sins are second only to murder in the category of personal crimes. (See Joseph F. Smith, *Gospel Doctrine,* p. 309.)

For those who have become entangled in the sins of immorality, President Benson counseled, "There is no choice but to repair your lives and repent of your sins. . . . Let your priesthood leaders help you resolve the transgression and come back into full fellowship with the Lord." (Devotional Address, BYU, October 13, 1987.) Take your concerns to your bishop. He will help you resolve your problems and show you how to gain forgiveness.

Only as we remain morally clean and pure can we

• Partake of the sacrament, have full fellowship in the Church, and have the blessings and spirit of the Lord to be with us always. (See 3 Nephi 18:28–29.)

• Receive and exercise the sacred powers of the holy priesthood and serve and magnify our callings in the Church. (See D&C 121:36–46; see also Robert L. Backman, *Ensign,* November 1989, pp. 38–40.)

• Enter the holy temple to receive our endowments and perform vicarious ordinances for the redemption of the dead. (See D&C 97:15–17.)

• Participate in missionary work or the gathering of the elect and the establishment of Zion. (See D&C 50:26–29; see also Ezra Taft Benson, "To Young Men of the Priesthood," pp. 6–7.)

• Be sealed to a worthy companion and participate in eternal family life. (See D&C 131:1–3; 132:19–22; see also

Boyd K. Packer, "Why Stay Morally Clean," *Ensign*, July 1972, pp. 111–13.)

• Be "fit and pure vessels to bear triumphantly the responsibilities of the kingdom of God in preparation for the second coming of our Savior." (*For the Strength of Youth*, pp. 4–5.)

• Be true to our God, ourselves, our sacred covenants, those we love, and those who love us, and be true to the unborn children who await and deserve a worthy and noble birthright. (See Boyd K. Packer, "Covenants," *Ensign*, November 1990, pp. 84–86.)

• Come to know and experience true love and everlasting happiness. (See Alma 38:12; Romans 13:10; Mosiah 2:41.)

Surely we can see that "sexual purity is youth's most precious possession; it is the foundation of all righteousness." (James R. Clark, ed., *Messages of the First Presidency*, [Salt Lake City: Bookcraft, 1975], 6:150) and "the very key to our happiness" and progression. Surely we can see also that sexual immorality is "service to Satan," (Spencer W. Kimball, *The Miracle of Forgiveness* [Salt Lake City: Bookcraft, 1969], p. 20) and only leads to sorrow, shame, guilt, broken hearts, broken dreams, and bondage (see Mosiah 2:32–40).

May you choose to obey the voice of the Lord and his servants! Choose to obey the eternal law of chastity or sexual purity! Choose to be fit and worthy vessels to bear off the responsibilities and qualify for the wonderful blessings of the kingdom of God in preparation for the coming of our Savior!

*Elder John M. Madsen, a member of the Seventy, has been an associate professor of ancient scripture at Brigham Young University. He graduated with a bachelor's degree from Washington State University and holds both a master's and a doctorate in educational psychology from BYU. He has worked as a teacher and an administrator in the Church Educational System and has served as a full-time mission president, a member of the Young Men general board, and a regional representative.*

## Chapter Twelve

# SUNDAY BEHAVIOR

Kathleen Lubeck

When I was a little girl seven years old, a girlfriend invited me to see a movie at a theater with her family—on Sunday. I don't remember who the friend was or what the show was. But I do remember talking to my mother about the invitation. What should I tell my friend?

"All I can tell you is what Heavenly Father has told us," my mother said. "The Sabbath is not like the other days of the week. It's his day. It's a day to go to church and to show our love to him and others. He wants us to keep it holy."

I understood what she was explaining. And then she taught me about choice and accountability: "But it's your decision whether to go or not. You know what the Lord has told us about Sunday. You decide what you should do."

Do you want to know what I did? I think you can guess. Even though I was only in the second grade and was far from being the perfect little girl, I wanted to do what the Lord asked. And I remember a warm feeling welling up within me, because my mother trusted me to make the decision.

The principle of keeping the Sabbath day holy has been with us since the creation of the world, when God rested from all his work on the seventh day. "God blessed the seventh day, and sanctified it: because that in it he had rested from all his work which God created and made." (Genesis 2:3.) He designated it a sacred day, dedicated to the worship of God, setting a pattern for all of humanity to follow.

Some of us follow it better than others. A great many distractions call to us, many of them activities that would keep us from devoting the Sabbath to worship. But despite the actions of some, it is a holy day, one which we are commanded by God to keep holy. A commandment is not simply advice or counsel. It is a direct imperative from God, which needs to be taken very seriously.

Along with the commandment, Heavenly Father has also given us the gift of agency, which allows us to make our own decisions about exactly how we're going to keep the Sabbath holy. It's obvious that some activities are inappropriate, like shopping, going water skiing or snow skiing, cleaning the garage or washing the car, or attending a concert or going to an amusement park.

But some people have legitimate questions about what is appropriate for that day. By giving us principles instead of spelling out every "do" or "don't" to us, Heavenly Father gives us the opportunity to draw closer to the Spirit and seek inspiration about what's appropriate if we aren't sure. Our decision-making process can become a teaching moment with the Spirit, as we offer our hearts to keep the Sabbath holy in full measure. Listening to the Spirit is essential.

One group of teens decided that they wanted to dress in shorts and go hiking in the mountains after their church meetings. They would take their scriptures with them, they said, so it would be an "appropriate" Sunday activity.

What they didn't ask was if it were a reverent way of honoring the Sabbath. Or if their attire was in keeping with the spirit of the Lord's honored day. Or if they were really in a situation to have the spirit of the Lord with them. Or if their example would have a positive impact on younger people who looked up to them.

There are many activities that would pull us away from the Spirit on Sunday. It's a good general rule to stay away from activities that you aren't quite sure are appropriate for the Sabbath.

For many people, the Sabbath has become a day like any other day of the week. For some it's a day to work and make money. (There is a difference between *choosing* to work on the Sabbath and *having* to work on the Sabbath.) To others, it's a day to spend money. What they don't realize is that these activities deprive them of Sabbath blessings that could be a part of their lives. "The Lord has given the Sabbath day for your benefit," we're told by the First Presidency in the pamphlet *For the*

*Strength of Youth.* Even though we're honoring the Sabbath day and obeying the Lord, it's for our benefit.

How does it benefit us? In many ways.

By honoring the Sabbath, we take time from our often very busy schedules to slow down and think about what's really important. A day each week is set aside for us to reflect on our blessings, return thanks to our Heavenly Father, think about the Savior, our love for him and his sacrifice for us, and to repent of our failings. Partaking of the sacrament provides an opportunity for reflection on a regular basis. As we participate, we think about what it means to be willing to take his name upon us and to promise to always remember him, that we may have his Spirit to be with us. The Sabbath gives us time to draw close to him in many other ways too, whether through sacred music, thinking about our lives and blessings, writing in our journals, reading the scriptures, or doing his work through visiting and helping others.

When you show your love to the Lord by obeying his commandments, you find a peace, even in the midst of outward turmoil. Most of us can use that kind of spiritual refreshment. By obeying God's commandments, we in a sense join "his team." We become his workers, yet (paradoxically) we find rest and inner peace. "Take my yoke upon you . . . and ye shall find rest unto your souls." (Matthew 11:29.)

The Sabbath provides us with an opportunity to spend time with our families, a feat that seems more and more difficult these days. I have wonderful personal memories of spending time with my parents and brothers and sisters on Sundays, doing things that built family relationships and that brought us all closer together.

It also gives us time to help other people. How many of us have the desire to help others, but just don't seem to find time to do so? My father is a doctor, and I remember him taking our family to visit some of his elderly patients in their homes on Sunday. He taught us some wonderful gospel principles about caring and service through his actions.

As we keep the Sabbath holy, we are showered with many blessings. That's what happens when we keep the Lord's commandments.

What are some of the principles about the Sabbath that we learn in *For the Strength of Youth*? (See pp. 16–17.) Here are just a few:

*Sunday dress:* "Your dress before and after meetings should reflect your respect for the Sabbath."

*Working on the Sabbath:* "When seeking a job, you may wish to share with your potential employer your desire to attend your Sunday meetings and keep the Sabbath holy. Many employers value employees with these personal convictions. Try to choose a job that doesn't require you to work on Sunday."

*Appropriate activities:* "Many activities are appropriate for the Sabbath; however, it is not a holiday. You should avoid seeking entertainment or spending money on this day."

Keeping the Sabbath holy is not so much an act as an attitude. The Lord tells us, "Draw near unto me and I will draw near unto you." (D&C 88:63.) That process of drawing near to the Lord, of worshipping him on this day, of offering our hearts and minds to him will bless our lives. It is a way of sanctifying our lives, turning them over to the Lord so he can make us clean. "Therefore, sanctify yourselves that your minds become single to God, and the days will come that you shall see him." (D&C 88:68.) May we reverence the Lord by keeping his Sabbath day holy, and be grateful for the blessings that come from keeping that commandment.

*Kathleen Lubeck has served as a member of the Young Women general board. She has been Director of National Media Placement in the Church Public Affairs Department. Sister Lubeck is a writer and has served as a Sunday School teacher, as a Relief Society teacher, and on the general Activities Committee of the Church.*

# Chapter Thirteen

▼ ▼ ▼

# SPIRITUAL HELP

Carolyn J. Rasmus

O ne of the best things about my calling is that I
have lots of opportunities to be with youth. I
love your enthusiasm and energy, your excitement for
life, and your fun-loving ways. I love to play and laugh
with you.

If I had one wish, it would be that each of you would
be happy and confident, that you'd feel good about who
you are and what you're doing. But as I've visited with
many of you, I sense your struggles and questions. I know
that many of you feel alone and unsure of yourselves.
Some of you wonder if you have a testimony and tell me
you've never felt the Spirit in your life.

I haven't always been a member of the Church, so a
lot of things I did when I was younger didn't seem wrong
to me. Many times in high school I went along with my
friends so they'd accept me and so I'd be part of the

group. If I knew then what I know now, I'm sure I would have done some things differently.

Because of these experiences and what I've learned since becoming a member of the Church, I'm anxious to share something that helps me now and that would have made all the difference when I was a teenager. I believe it's one of the most important things anyone can know. It's simply — we're not alone. There is always help available.

In the *For the Strength of Youth* wallet-size supplement, the First Presidency has written: "Spiritual Help: You are never alone. Rely on the Holy Ghost. Knowing what is right and wrong is always possible." I've memorized these three sentences. They come to my mind frequently — especially when I feel afraid, alone, unsure, or wonder what I should do in certain situations.

Before joining the Church, I didn't know very much about the Spirit even though I'd been taught by the missionaries. I'd been reading the Book of Mormon and praying, but I didn't have any idea if the Church was true. Lots of things sounded right to me, and I felt good when I went to church meetings. A friend suggested that I fast to know if the Church was true. I agreed.

I was studying for a test at school. About the time I would have eaten breakfast, I found I couldn't concentrate. Finally, I decided to pray. As I asked Heavenly Father to help me, the following words came into my mind: "Go now, my child, for there is much work to be done. I send my Spirit to be with you to enable you to work and think clearly, to accomplish all that lies before you. Later return unto me, coming to me with real intent of prayer."

After this happened, I felt peaceful and was able to study. About lunchtime I took a break, and while I was looking at the mountains, I had another experience. It was like a voice inside my head telling me to read Doctrine and Covenants 89. When I read this scripture about the Word of Wisdom, I decided never to drink coffee again.

Later that day I went into a room by myself to pray. I wanted to know if the Church was really true. I didn't expect to see a vision, but I believed something would happen. I waited a long time—nothing happened. But I couldn't forget about the Church and the good feelings I had when I read the scriptures or was with my Latter-day Saint friends. Finally, I decided to be baptized. I wasn't sure I had a testimony, but it seemed like the right thing to do.

Now, twenty years later, I know that I did the right thing, and I have a testimony that the Church is true. I've also learned about the Spirit and how it works. In the Book of Mormon, Enos tells us that while he was praying, "The voice of the Lord came into [his] mind." (Enos 1:10.) That's what happened to me the day I fasted. The Lord was talking to me through the Spirit by putting thoughts into my mind. The Lord answered my prayer, but because I didn't understand how the Spirit works, I "missed the message" and assumed that God wasn't listening and didn't answer my prayer.

The scriptures have helped me understand why I felt good when I was with my new friends. The Apostle Paul tells us that the "fruit of the Spirit" includes love, joy, peace, gentleness, goodness, and faith. (See Galatians

5:22.) These are the feelings I had when I was with my friends, and it made me feel good. I also know why joining the Church seemed like the right thing to do. "The Spirit of the Lord . . . wrought a mighty change in [me]." (Mosiah 5:2), and I wanted to do what was right.

The First Presidency has said that you have been born at a time "when the temptations, responsibilities, and opportunities are the very greatest." (*For the Strength of Youth,* p. 3.) They have also promised that the Holy Ghost "can help you make good choices" and "help you know right from wrong." (*For the Strength of Youth,* p. 17.)

I believe you do know what is right. You have been taught by your parents and church leaders; you have guidelines explained in *For the Strength of Youth.* Then why do some youth struggle with dishonesty, use crude language and vulgarity, and even tamper with Satanism? Why are some tempted by drugs or the desire to engage in sexual relations before marriage?

Christ explained this to the Nephites. He said, "Satan desireth to have you." (3 Nephi 18:18.) Satan will do everything possible to keep us from returning to our Heavenly Father. Satan makes evil things look enticing, attractive, and pleasurable as he tries to persuade us to follow him instead of Christ. He is clever. He wants us to rationalize our behavior and believe that disobeying the commandments isn't a serious thing. This is a lie! It is one of the ways Satan deceives us.

But God does not leave us alone to battle with Satan. He has given us the gift of the Holy Ghost. When we remember Christ and keep his commandments, God promises that we will always have his Spirit to be with us. It is through his Spirit that we will have the courage, the strength, the power, and the self-discipline to choose good over evil, right over wrong.

I believe there are three things that can help you have his Spirit in your life:

1. *Pray.* When you are tempted or need to make an important decision, ask the Lord for inspiration. Then listen for the influence of his Spirit and follow those promptings. Often good thoughts and ideas will come into your mind and you will feel peaceful.

2. *Read the scriptures.* Sometimes when I read the scriptures, I feel there is a message just for me. That is one of the ways our Heavenly Father teaches us. As you read the scriptures, you will grow closer to our Heavenly Father. Often you will feel his Spirit as you read.

3. *Keep the commandments.* When you keep God's commandments you will experience the guidance of his Spirit. Laman and Lemuel didn't obey the commandments; they were "past feeling" and couldn't "feel" the words of the Spirit. (1 Nephi 17:45.) When you're obedient, you qualify yourself to receive blessings and inspiration from God. (See D&C 130:20–21.)

The Spirit works in different ways with different people. You might not hear a voice in your head or "feel" an impression in your mind as I did, but the Spirit can bless you with feelings of peace, joy, and well-being. I know from my own experience that the Holy Ghost can help you make right choices. When challenged or tempted, remember—you're not alone. The Holy Ghost will help you know right from wrong. Spiritual help is always available. As you pray, read the scriptures, and keep the commandments, you will grow in confidence and feel good about yourself. You will be guided by his Spirit and be able to accomplish your righteous desires.

*Carolyn J. Rasmus serves as an administrative assistant to the Young Women general presidency. She holds an Ed.D. from BYU and has served as executive assistant to two presidents of Brigham Young University. Sister Rasmus has held numerous teaching positions in the Church, including gospel doctrine teacher, and has served as a ward and stake Young Women president.*

Chapter Fourteen

▼ ▼ ▼

# REPENTANCE

Bruce C. Hafen and
Marie K. Hafen

Why do you kids act like there's a war on?" a frustrated old man once yelled at some hyperactive teenagers. Well, there is a war on—the great war between good and evil is in its final stages. The Evil One has dragged out his deadliest weapons, including "biological" and "chemical" warfare. Amid this battle, we look for instructions, not only on how to survive, but how to win the war.

Like a leaflet of freedom dropped literally from above, the First Presidency has sent us an urgent spiritual survival kit: *For the Strength of Youth.* It is a message of happiness and hope. As Elder Boyd K. Packer once said, "Oh, youth, if you could know! The requirements of the Church are the highway to love and to happiness, with guardrails securely in place, with guideposts plainly marked, and with help along the way. How unfortunate to resent counsel and restraint! How fortunate are you who follow the standards of the Church, even if just from sheer obedience or habit! You will find a rapture and a joy fulfilled." (*Let Not Your Heart Be Troubled* [Salt Lake City: Bookcraft, 1991], p. 140.)

But this message is also a voice of warning and a call to repentance. It is a stirring wake-up call, like trumpets in the dawn, lest the moral nerve gas that surrounds us claim any more into that deadly slumber from which none can awaken.

*For the Strength of Youth* teaches about repentance with new insight, warning us that Satan is manipulating the very concept of repentance: "Some people knowingly break God's commandments. They plan to repent before they go on a mission or receive the sacred covenants and ordinances of the temple." (*For the Strength of Youth*, p. 17.)

There is something especially perverse about "planning to repent" in the very act of transgression. This is twisting a sublime source of healing to make it actually inflict more sickness, like poisoning the medicine in the hospital for wounded soldiers. "Woe unto them that call evil good, and good evil." (Isaiah 5:20.) But in the great war, Satan isn't bound by the rules of fair play.

This kind of thinking can begin early. We know two brothers whom we'll call Steve and Scott, ages nine and seven. Steve had been baptized; Scott would be baptized soon. One day their father found that Scott had taken a dollar that did not belong to him. As they sat down to talk about the seriousness of stealing, Scott was at first very penitent. Then he looked up brightly and said, "But Dad, Steve says it's okay to steal things until you're eight!" The startled father then asked Steve, his young theologian, why he would have said such a thing. Steve replied confidently, "That's what I told him. When he's eight, he'll be baptized, and all his sins will be washed away. So I say, live it up!"

Sometimes young people preparing to attend a Church college, to go on a mission, or to be married in the temple will consciously "live it up," as if they have a license to sin all they wish, so long as they "just repent" before the deadline. Paul described these foolish ones as wanting "to enjoy the pleasures of sin for a season." (Hebrews 11:25.) Some even feel it is their "right" to romp in the mud of transgression right up to the moment they take their spiritual shower of repentance.

Sadly, those who walk too close to the edge of a penalty-free romping time may discover too late that they cannot wash every stain from their clothes and hands. Of course repentance, when it is genuine and complete, can restore our spiritual standing before God. But even then, the entanglements of sin (see D&C 88:86) — the bent fenders and the broken hearts, the addictions and the lost opportunities, the unwanted children and the unfortunate marriages, the bills to pay and the fences to mend — these consequences may never wash away.

Moreover, once sin's swift current carries us downstream, we can't always just turn around at will and swim back, against the current, to our point of beginning. We don't have that much control over our lives. One of the most exciting football games in BYU history was the so-called "Miracle Bowl" in 1980 against SMU. The Cougars were behind four touchdowns with only minutes to play. Then, amazingly, they came roaring back to win the game with an onside kick and a "hail Mary" pass in the final seconds.

The next year in an early game, BYU fell far behind against a very tough team. Our ten-year-old daughter said, "You know, this is a lot more fun for everybody — let the other team get way ahead, and then just pass them up like we did last year!" But it wasn't to be — the Cougars were soundly defeated, and our daughter had to rethink her philosophy about coming from behind.

The deadly AIDS epidemic illustrates the tragedy of ignoring the consequences of sin. For example, some American athletes and entertainers have been stunned to discover that, because of their sexual promiscuity, they are now infected with the virus from which AIDS can develop. According to published estimates, some of these traveling celebrities have had sexual encounters with literally hundreds of different partners in city after city. Now they are discovering that their carefree life-style may cost them their lives. And beyond that, they may have unwittingly infected their spouses and children — those who mean the most to them. But now, even if they were to repent, there is no way to call back the seeds of destruction they have scattered in their past.

James foresaw the misery of such sad wanderers: "We will go into such a city, and continue there a year, and buy and sell, and get gain: whereas ye know not what shall be on the morrow. For what is your life? It is even a vapour, that appeareth for a little time, and then vanisheth away."(James 4:13–14.)

Yet many today still tell America's youth that they can "live it up" and avoid such fates as AIDS if they just practice "safe sex." But any sex outside marriage is by definition unsafe, physically and spiritually. "Safe sex" is as self-contradictory as "benign terminal illness." A fastened seat belt does not make it safe to drive 150 mph. *Living* that fast will never be "safe." And the father of lies certainly knows that.

Finally, "planning to repent" is an affront to the Savior, because it assumes that we control our own forgiveness. While we must do "all we can do" (2 Nephi 25:23) to be worthy of Christ's grace, we cannot turn that miraculous power on and off like a water faucet. He *loves* us no matter what we do, but he *forgives* only the honest in heart, and on his terms, not ours.

Because we lack both the power and ability to compensate fully for the effects of our sins, we are utterly dependent on Jesus Christ. Without his holy atonement, no amount of agonizing repentance could cleanse and return us to God's presence. We dare not trifle with so sacred a reality. But the good news is that when we do fully repent in the honesty of a broken heart and a contrite spirit, he will do all the rest. Thank God, literally, *that* is under *his* control — not ours, for *only he* has the power to make our scarlet sins be white as snow. (See Isaiah 1:18.)

*Bruce C. Hafen, BYU provost and professor of law, was previously president of Ricks College. Brother Hafen is the author of several church books and has served in a bishopric, as a high councilor, in a stake presidency, and as a regional representative.*

*Marie K. Hafen has been a member of the Young Women general board. She has taught English and literature on a college level. In the Church, Sister Hafen has been a Relief Society president and teacher, a Young Women president and adviser, and a member of the General Relief Society Curriculum Committee. The Hafens are the parents of seven children.*

Chapter Fifteen

# WORTHINESS
# AND SERVICE

Elder V. Dallas Merrell

The inspired booklet *For the Strength of Youth* reveals this truth: "Joy and happiness come from living the way the Lord wants you to live and from service to God and others." (P. 19.) Our ability and worthiness to serve are dependent upon being obedient. This takes discipline.

The media tell us daily about the success of highly disciplined people. Much of what the world considers to be important in this life results from disciplined effort— whether it be in academics, careers, athletics, or entertainment. Greater than any worldly accomplishments are being worthy and able to serve the Lord. Those who would serve God must do so with all their "heart, might, mind and strength." (D&C 4:2.) Again, in the Church, discipline, worthiness, and service go together. I learned an unforgettable lesson about this from a horse named Champ.

I first saw Champ at a remote Idaho ranch on a wintry day when I was eleven years old. A cowboy roped the black yearling, his first encounter with man. My heart raced as Dad bought this wild beauty. He fought intensely as we loaded him into the truck to take him home. Champ was coal black, marked with a white stripe down his nose and white stocking feet. He had an extraordinary lineage. His maternal grandfather was Man O' War of Kentucky, the most famous race horse of all time, the largest money winner in the history of horse racing, and a sire with more race-winning offspring than any horse that had lived.

Champ was carefully trained, first with a rope around his neck, a gunnysack on his back, then a saddle, and finally a young boy astride him. I loved him. A real partnership blossomed between the horse and this boy, herding milk cows and driving away range cattle to protect our crops. Champ became a disciplined ally, a valuable servant to his master, and a great friend. I would often ride Champ without saddle or bridle—just the two of us in unity, racing at breakneck speed, enjoying the blazing paces that were the product of his genes. A subtle touch on his neck was his command. A shift in my posture would slow him down or speed him up. He was totally obedient. We were one.

Champ's reputation grew as he carried rodeo queens and became grand champion at the county fair. Then he disappeared. He was gone when we came home from church after dark, and we assumed he was obscured in a nearby field, being as black as the night itself. But the morning did not disclose his whereabouts. We called and searched everywhere. Eventually, we concluded that Champ had been stolen.

I couldn't accept Champ being gone. In defiance of the obvious, I recruited a cousin and we rode into the wastelands well beyond our farm where I had seen wild horses. After hours of riding, we were close to despair when we detected some form on the horizon and discovered that, indeed, there were horses ahead. The wild horses raced far ahead of us, but after extensive maneuvering we surprised them from a low-lying area. To our amazement, the errant black stood majestically in full view with about twenty other startled steeds. With heads high and tails flying, they burst away for another chase. Champ led the pack. Controlled by his environment, he was as wild as the first day I saw him.

What a contrast! We were not racing on the manicured track in the Kentucky Derby where Champ's grandfather was famous. We were in uncharted territory, endangered by rocky terrain, and in the race of our lives. The future of this horse of grand lineage was at stake. I was determined to bring him home.

We eventually forced the steaming horses over a steep hill, into our valley, and onto the dirt road that passed our home. The horses thundered beyond our place, but we cornered them in a neighbor's pasture. Champ and a mare bolted through a fence, but finally we captured him in our corral.

Dad reached Champ first, eased up to him, and embraced him as only a horse lover would understand. The prized Champ was back home where he belonged with

THE FIGHT FOR RIGHT

his master, retrieved from the freedom that would have destroyed him. For not long after Champ's return, his roving companions were rounded up and processed as dog food. Without our timely rescue, Champ would have been wasted with them.

Champ's worth to his master was dependent upon his willingness to serve — upon the commitment of his "heart, might, mind and strength" being available and obedient to his master's call. Service in the Lord's kingdom, likewise, is a partnership with our Master, Jesus Christ, requiring that we love and follow him. The First Presidency, in *For the Strength of Youth,* has provided us with specific guidelines for being worthy and more able to serve the Lord throughout our lives. They include the following:

1. *Dating.* By following this counsel you will remain morally clean but will also learn more about various people, develop your social skills, build respect for your standards and abilities, and establish a strong foundation for future service and leadership in the kingdom.

2. *Dress and appearance.* One who serves effectively must have a good image and win the confidence of others. How you look will shape future opportunities because the Lord will be able to take advantage of your other qualities.

3. *Friendshipping.* Everyone wants to have friends and to be a friend. Service often is rendered to those who are our friends, in wards, stakes, and neighborhoods. As you treat people kindly and feel genuine concern for their well-being, you will more naturally render valuable service.

4. *Honesty.* Service generally involves having a relationship of trust with people. Honesty with yourself and others is a bedrock requirement for a true servant.

5. *Language.* Foul and inappropriate language turns away others who need our service and love. We must not only avoid unworthy language, but also improve our capacity for leadership and service by learning to communicate thoughts and feelings with well-chosen words and actions.

6. *Media.* Much good is accomplished through contemporary media — we learn of lands, histories, cultures, personalities, technology, current events, science. By avoiding degrading television, literature, and movies, and by taking advantage of the positive, you will avoid pitfalls and enhance your potential to serve the Lord.

7. *Mental and physical health.* You cannot serve your God and others effectively without a clear mind, emotions that are in control, and a body that works. Do not place unnecessary limitations on your future by abusing yourself.

8. *Live worthy of the Spirit.* Lift your soul with good music, wholesome recreation, virtuous conduct, Sabbath worship, companionship of the Holy Ghost, and proper repentance. True charity and Christlike service are built on these forms of discipline and preparation.

I pray that each of us will recognize the need to become disciplined and responsive under the loving reins of our Church leaders and that we will be worthy to serve by avoiding life's wastelands. Only when we can respond to the subtle promptings of the Spirit, as Champ did to the light touch of my hand, can we become an instrument in the Lord's hands and work together as one.

*V. Dallas Merrell, a member of the Seventy, has authored books on leadership and management. He earned his bachelor's and master's degrees from BYU and his doctorate from the University of Southern California. His professional career was in the field of corporate development. Elder Merrell has served as a full-time mission president and as a regional representative.*

▼ ▼ ▼

# INDEX

# INDEX

Hafen, Bruce C., 88
Hafen, Marie K., 88
Handel, 51
Happiness, appearance of, in
  beer commercials, 1–2
Hate, 66
Health: hazards to, 2; spiritual,
  32; mental and physical,
  43–47, 93
Heavenly Father: covenant
  people of, 7–8; reverence
  owed to, 34; spiritual
  instruction from, 47;
  instructions from, on
  Sabbath, 71–74; assists us in
  battle with Satan, 80
Hill Cumorah, 51
Holy Ghost, 4, 78, 80
Homes, broken, causes of, 37
Homosexuality, 40, 64
Honesty: lack of, in world, 3; in
  filing insurance claim, 26–27;
  promotes self-esteem, 28; as
  measure of character, 29; as
  basis of trusting
  relationships, 30; as
  requirement for service, 93
Honor, 28
House of Israel, 8
Hymns used in Lord's work, 50

Immorality, problems of, 3, 40,
  65–66, 87. See also Sexual
  sins
Incest, 64
Influence on others, 23, 73
Integrity, 28

Intimacy, 10

Jealousy, 66
Jesus Christ: sacrificed himself
  for sin, 4; sets standards of
  righteousness, 5; condemns
  vile speech, 32; reverence
  owed to, 34; endured our
  pains, 44; invites all to come
  unto him, 47; birth of, 50;
  second coming of, 50, 68;
  remembered on the Sabbath,
  74; sin an affront to, 87
Jokes, off-color, 32, 41
Journal keeping, 74
Joy, obedience results in, 4, 44
Judgment impaired by beer
  drinking, 2

Kapp, Ardeth G., 12
Kimball, Spencer W., 40
Kindness, 21
Kingdom of God, 5, 64, 68
Kuwait, example of, 38

Language, 31–35, 93
Lewdness, 41
Lubeck, Kathleen, 76
Lying, 30

Madsen, John M., 69
Maeser, Karl G., 27
Man O' War, horse named, 90
Marriage, 65; eternal, 8–9, 12,
  21
Masturbation, 64
McConkie, Bruce R., 54–55
McKay, David O., 23

97

# INDEX

# INDEX